IMAGES
of England

BROMSGROVE

The Horn and Trumpet on the Kidderminster Road in the early years of this century.

IMAGES
of England

BROMSGROVE

Compiled by
Margaret Cooper

TEMPUS

First published 1998
Reprinted 1999, 2001
Copyright © Margaret Cooper, 1998

Tempus Publishing Limited
The Mill, Brimscombe Port,
Stroud, Gloucestershire, GL5 2QG

ISBN 0 7524 1146 2

Typesetting and origination by
Tempus Publishing Limited
Printed in Great Britain by
Midway Colour Print, Wiltshire

Contents

A 'Light Dray, suitable for Brewers or Bottlers', made by the coach builder, Daniel Giles, a century ago at his workshop in Station Street. Notice the price of a dozen bottles of Ansells' ales.

Introduction

A century ago the people of Bromsgrove were really no different from us: they ate and slept, worked and played, went to school, did the shopping, looked forward to holidays and special events, attended church, drank at the local and, just like us, had their good and bad days, their ups and downs. The *details* of their lives, however, were often very different from ours and the backdrop to their daily comings and goings has now been radically altered.

An interesting snapshot of Bromsgrove and its inhabitants exactly one hundred years ago can be developed from *Palmer's Almanack and Directory*. Alfred Palmer was the former partner of Benjamin Maund, the distinguished botanist and bookseller in the High Street, and he began publishing his series of directories shortly before bringing out the first edition of the *Bromsgrove and Droitwich Weekly Messenger* in January 1860. As well as general information about the town, the directory lists the residents, their occupations and their addresses. Several points stand out in the 1898 edition. To begin with, the High Street was clearly the province of the private family trader. Businesses were owned – and still usually lived above – by local families who knew the town and their customers and who, for the most part, kept on working until they died. The shops were often smaller than today's 'retail outlets' (and the photographs show how goods were packed into every square inch of window, both inside and out, a far cry from today's favoured minimalism); but there were many more of them. In the High Street alone, for example, there were ten grocers, nine tailors/drapers and five bakers. When this is widened to take in the town centre as a whole these figures leap to sixteen tailors/drapers, fourteen grocers and fourteen bakers. A further fourteen names were categorized as 'shopkeepers', men and women who probably sold a variety of goods.

There was the usual range of shops, of course – half a dozen tobacconists, nine butchers, three chemists, four furniture dealers – but there were also the kinds of shops that have long disappeared – a couple of tea merchants, four milliners and a straw hat and bonnet maker, four corn and seed merchants, an oil dealer, two sellers of musical instruments, a dealer in soot and, envious thought, three fishmongers. To make ends meet, no doubt, many shopkeepers added other strings to their bows, like John Satchwell, a fishmonger as well as a blacksmith, and Mrs Sarah Johnson who ran a registry office for servants in addition to making and selling brushes.

Perhaps the most striking feature of the directory, however, is the overall picture it gives of the town centre. At the very heart of Bromsgrove were not just the many and varied shops. This was the place where things were manufactured and crafted, where a great range of services were provided and where people actually lived – not just above and behind their premises but in private houses. The centre of the town was where everything happened, where people visited the doctor or the dentist or the vet (almost all of them in the High Street itself), got their hair cut (at one of four hairdressers), ordered coal, engaged the services of a solicitor, an estate agent, a carpenter, a plumber, a market gardener, a chimney sweep, a stonemason, a carrier, a laundress and, if times were hard, a pawnbroker (only one officially listed, although others almost certainly operating 'informally'). And here too was where things were made: agricultural implements and ironmongery, nails (the old staple industry fast declining but still of some significance), coaches, carriages and carts, clothes (four dressmakers – but also, by this stage, two sewing machine agents), hats, saddles and other leather goods, watches and clocks, bikes (two cycle makers), barrels, furniture, wheels and beer ('Fitch's celebrated mild and bitter ales and stout', made in the brewery behind Worcester Street, were enjoyed in local hostelries like the Cattle Market Tavern).

In stark contrast to today's town centre there is an almost unnerving absence of the financial services that now have such a foothold in High Streets all over the country. In 1898 there were just two banks, one insurance agent – although insurance could be arranged through other businesses like *The Messenger* and Alfred Dipple, the estate agent – and an accountant who was also secretary to the Bromsgrove Gas Company.

It all seems light years away from today's town centre where hardly anything is made, shops are fewer and less varied and consumers are enticed on to the outskirts where parking is guaranteed and most of the week's needs available under one roof. The idea of breaking up the centre of this old town would have been greeted with bewilderment a century ago, followed probably by the thought that there was enough walking already.

Two particular types of occupation have not yet been mentioned but these directory entries alone tell us so much about how things were in 1898. There were thirteen makers of boots and shoes (mostly boots) and five blacksmiths for a population that went everywhere by 'Shanks's pony' unless they were fortunate enough to own the real thing, in which case the horses would do the work.

This selection of photographs highlights some of these overall changes. In particular we see a kind of street life most of us have never experienced, children playing in the Worcester Road, people standing in the middle of the High Street chatting, endless local groups and organizations processing for one reason or another, crowds gathering for election speeches, town hall announcements and coronation celebrations. There is the assumption that the highways were theirs, a natural extension of their living space, especially for those whose homes were dark and cramped. This was a time when the motorcar and the motor omnibus were barely on the horizon.

The photographs also show how dependent the community still was on the working horse. They were a vital part of everyday life, carrying their riders, pulling gigs and carriages and hauling the goods of many of Bromsgrove's businesses. At this stage Palmer's directories regularly carried large advertisements for insuring horses and cattle, and pubs like the Roebuck Inn and Posting House advertised their 'Broughams, Landaus, Waggonettes, Dog Carts, Brakes' and 'good horses, steady and efficient drivers'.

The annual midsummer fair, granted to the town by King John in 1199, still attracted great throngs and an equally great 'assemblage of horses, mules and donkeys ... ponies who wore ear-caps fringed with tinkling bells ... great shire and cart horses, their brasses shining like gold in the sun, their manes and tails plaited and tied with bright-hued ribbons and the flowers of the field'. Then there were the horses and ponies up for sale, tethered in the pound in Church Street where they had been relocated in the 1850s when High Street showing and selling had become too dangerous (and messy!).

The fair and the regular cattle market meant there were few who were not used to the sight, sound and smell of farm animals, and few who did not have some contact with the farmers, smallholders and market gardeners who worked on the town's edges and in the surrounding villages and brought their produce into Bromsgrove. On market days around the turn of the century one of these smallholders used to walk from Clattercut Lane into Bromsgrove, a round trip of about nine miles, with several of her children helping to carry her baskets of fresh vegetables and fruit. The horse fair, the regular cattle auctions and the sale of local produce direct to the customer were the hallmarks of the market town Bromsgrove had been for centuries. And the local inns, twenty-seven of them listed in the 1898 directory, did good business in all this, providing food and drink for the farmers and market gardeners, stabling their horses and putting up their floats.

In these digital and e-mail times, we may be hard put to imagine what people found to do all those years ago outside their working day. The simple answer is plenty. Documentary evidence would reveal even more, but there are enough examples in these photographs alone to show that late-Victorian Bromsgrovians did not need to stay at home twiddling their thumbs. Children played out in safer streets, had fun at the open-air swimming baths, went to the fair and on family outings, watched a match and picked strawberries. For adults there were all sorts of possibilities. The sporting scene was already well organized: apart from the Rovers (founded in 1885), there were several other football teams. In addition, Bromsgrove Rugby Club was staging matches at its ground in the town centre and Bromsgrove Cricket Club playing its matches on the Recreation Ground. There were tennis, hockey and bowls clubs and some organizations, like the police force, already had their own sports clubs. Cycling was enjoying huge popularity as some pictures show and several local establishments offered accommodation for those on bikes.

For the less sporty – or the all-rounder – there was a newly formed drama society which performed at the Drill Hall, occasional dramatic offerings at the Corn Exchange and music hall, variety shows and more drama at the Assembly Rooms and Theatre. There was also a philharmonic society and a variety of art and craft classes at the Institute in New Road. It is a very curious thought that as Bromsgrove approaches the twenty-first century it has neither a cinema nor a theatre: eighty years ago it had two designated theatres and sixty years ago two cinemas.

Bromsgrove underwent some big changes in the 1960s, '70s and '80s when many buildings were knocked down – the Cottage Hospital, the Victorian Institute and School of Art and Science, the Stratford Road almshouses and numerous old cottages – changes which transformed areas like St John Street and Hanover Street. New roads were built, like that running west behind the High Street and the new eastern bypass. The cattle market, the last remaining feature of the old market town, was dismantled to make way for a supermarket; and the town's green edges, where once there were farms, were nibbled, then gobbled up for housing and industry. 'Yesterday's Bromsgrove' could be as close as the 1960s.

Of course, change is not only inevitable but necessary. Not all the demolished buildings were worth saving; but in the last fifty years too many have been knocked down with too little thought. The move towards restoring and preserving the best, such as the Mitre, the Golden Lion and Strand House, is more than timely, but holding on to what is best from the past, while meeting the needs of today's residents and their children, is quite a balancing act.

A decade ago, three sprightly eighty and ninety-year-olds were asked to look back on some of the changes they had seen. There was no united cry for the past, however; they were much too positive and realistic for that. Sidney Taylor, who came to Bromsgrove as a small boy in 1906 and retired from the family ironmongery business in the 1960s, felt that the town was a very great improvement on the 'slovenly and untidy' place he remembered it to be then. He spoke with real enthusiasm about improvements to Crown Close and the benefits of pedestrianization. Harriet Milne was born and bred in Bromsgrove, though she lived in Scotland for a number of years before returning in the late 1950s. She spoke fondly of 'the church school' in Crown Close, Mrs Biddle's sweet shop in the Worcester Road, her excellent training as a milliner and all the musical and sporting activities she was involved with as a teenager. However, she was philosophical about the changes, seeing them not as 'bad' but as necessary: 'People have got to be housed. I think we *should* try to keep Bromsgrove as a market town but I don't see how.' Elsie Cooper came from Birmingham in 1931 to settle in the 'friendly market town'. She lived on the route taken by the men who drove the cattle from the market to the station and recalled always having to make sure on market days that her gate was in good order and closed. Of all the changes, the best for her included the building of the swimming pool – 'so much pleasure for so many people' – and 'decent council houses ... much better than some of those old cottages which were really rather grim'. One thing all three regretted, however, was the demise of so many smaller shops:

'The High Street used to be full of small shops where you could get practically everything you needed.'

'That's the difference – it used to be all shops.'

'Gone are the delicatessens and grocers where you could slip in for a quarter of ham for your lunch.'

Acknowledgements

A little over a third of the photographs reproduced here come from Tim Brotherton's collection of more than seven hundred which he amassed over many years in the town. Tim's professional life, as an estate agent, put him in an ideal position to be able to rescue not just photographs but all kinds of material which might otherwise have been lost for ever, and the town is very much the richer for his efforts. Tim died at the end of last year but not before handing over the collection into safe hands and, since he was always generous with his time and his help, I think he would approve of the use to which a part of his collection is being put.

It is entirely due to the ready co-operation of so many Bromsgrovians, all named below, that the bulk of the pictures are assembled here. Many went to great lengths to dig out their family albums, dismantle framed photographs, identify forgotten relatives, write to friends no longer in the town and suggest further people to approach. The whole exercise has led to many interesting and humorous encounters and I hope they all feel it has been worth it.

Philip Amphlett, Roger Brazier, Shirley Brittan, Bromsgrove Baptist Church, Harvey and Ian Bryant (John Bryant & Sons), Ann Burdett, Barry Carpenter, Terry Carter, Hazel Chidley, Terry Clarke, Tony Cowan, Florence Crane, Peter Fielden (Bromsgrove School), Margaret Fishley, Joyce Gill, Horace Hall, Edna Harrison, Bernard Hirons, Matthew Horton (Thomas Horton & Sons, Solicitors), Gordon James, Betty Jones, Bill Kings, Zena Lambe, Jo Morgan, John Paul (Bromsgrove Rugby Club), Olive and Bernard Poulteney, Martin Powell (Victor Powell, Estate Agents), Mabel Rainscourt (Rainscourt Ltd), Tec Richards (Finstall First School), Sylvia and Bob Richardson, Brian Rutter, the late Bill Russell, Sheena Shirley, Pat Tansell, Margaret Wall, Mark Weaver (Weaver PLC, Building Contractors), Mike Webb, Audrey Wheeler, Max White, Janet Woodhall. I would also like to thank W. Eileen Davies for kindly allowing me to quote from her book *Seechem Chronicles*.

One
The Market Place

Hanover Street looking towards St John's Church in the early 1930s. Thirty years later virtually all the buildings in this interesting old street had gone.

The busy lower end of the High Street looking towards the Market Place, *c.* 1905. This was the old centre of Bromsgrove, where in past centuries labourers and servants were hired each September at the annual hiring fair, where wrongdoers were whipped, pilloried or put in the stocks and, still at this stage, the stalls of the open-air market were set up on market days. In the centre is the town hall, built in 1832 to replace a much older timber-framed building. The bank on the right – amazingly, unnamed – started as a private enterprise in 1852, then became a branch of the Stourbridge & Kidderminster Banking Co. and, after several mergers, the Midland Bank. Below the bank is the old *Messenger* office and shop. Between 1818 and 1859 the renowned botanist and horticulturalist Benjamin Maund ran his bookselling business from these premises and soon after he retired his former partner, Alfred Palmer, published the first edition of the *Bromsgrove and Droitwich Weekly Messenger* on 7 January 1860. The first shop on the left with the white globes was Henry Wiggan's, draper and hatter. At this stage the town was still very well supplied with makers and sellers of hats.

The Market Place in the late nineteenth century. The building in the centre was known as Roundabout House and, until its demolition in 1899 (see p. 107), made the entrance to St John Street very narrow. The 'Hallelujah Lamp', so called because the Salvation Army held meetings around it, stood on the site of the old stone market cross.

The removal of Roundabout House allowed this mid-1920s view to be taken of the bottom of the High Street and the narrow building on the left which is today's Market Place post office. In the centre is the west side of the town hall and on the right the George Hotel.

A photograph probably taken from Roundabout House looking up the High Street in the early 1890s. Below the Golden Cross are two grocers next door to each other. Billingham operated for nearly a quarter of a century; Burgis and Colbourne, a branch of the Leamington shop, had closed by 1900.

Forty years later and the most obvious change to the above scene is the arrival of the car which could still be parked more or less anywhere.

The Market Place in the early 1930s. The town hall has gone, knocked down in 1928 (see p. 109). Now nothing stands in front of the George Hotel, part of which can be seen on the right. The George was one of Bromsgrove's old inns, rebuilt in 1900 with its main entrance moved from Worcester Street to St John Street. It finally came down in the 1960s, making way for offices and shops. Another old hostelry, the Golden Lion, can be seen on the left – the building with the four distinctive ogee arches. It had served as a busy coaching inn on this site for over two centuries before closing in 1985; but this is one of the buildings to have been renovated in the last decade rather than knocked down. Further left is Bradley's, the clothes shop (whose ground floor until 1998 accommodated Bromsgrove Books), and next to it the Market Place café run by Thomas Kearn, a confectioner. This rather higgledy-piggledy roof line disappeared in the 1960s when alterations included a flat roof.

St John Street, *c.* 1907/8. A year or two later the plaster on the building to the right was removed, revealing the black and white building known for over half a century as Appleby's Corner (see p. 17). The little building at the back was the town's fire engine house.

St John Street in the late 1930s. To the right of the boy in the centre is the urinal with its lamp and elaborate Victorian cast-iron walls, straddling, not surprisingly, the Spadesbourne Brook. It is remembered as not quite the sweetest smelling part of town.

The corner of the High Street and St John Street, *c.* 1912. Four centuries ago a very fine four-gabled, timber-framed building stood here. In the last hundred years it has been eaten away, with a large one-and-a-quarter-gable chunk removed by Thomas Hall, the draper, who wanted his Manchester House to be double-fronted. Finally, in 1962, the St John Street end was replaced by a lower, flat-roofed building and Appleby's was bought by a building society and rebuilt.

No. 1 St John Street, next to the Spadesbourne bridge parapet, *c.* 1905. Walter Nokes, furniture remover and general grocer, moved here from Worcester Street in 1894. The young girls are Maud Amess (left) and Lily Nokes (right).

The south side of St John Street at the turn of the century. The double-fronted shop next but one to Nokes' premises is Carr's, Bromsgrove's oldest china and glass warehouse, established in the 1840s. On the ground floor at this stage it also sold brushes, brooms and baskets.

A closer view of No. 1 St John Street in 1925. In the doorway is Lily Nokes and her brother, Arthur. Twenty years on from the photograph on the previous page, it is interesting how much advertising the shop front is now displaying.

The Shoulder of Mutton Inn, kept at this stage by Matthew Jones, *c.* 1900. The cottages on the left were demolished in the 1950s. For many years before the Second World War, Steps Cottage, on the right, was the home of Miss Hannah Bridge and bore the sign 'District Midwife'. She was paid, before the National Health Service, by public subscription.

A turn-of-the-century view from St John's tower over the south east of the town. Dominating the upper centre of the picture are the buildings of Bromsgrove School, while the crowded cottages to the left of Hanover Street (fires blazing, washing on the line) have long gone. The site is now occupied by the market car park.

The top of Worcester Street in the early 1920s. The shop being altered stood next to Whitfield's, now Vine's (just visible on the near left). It was later demolished, giving Vine's a corner on to George Street. The poster on the back of the town hall is advertising Pola Negri, tempestuous star of the silent screen, in *Barbed Wire*.

John Lloyd, a substantial butcher, and his staff outside No. 2 Worcester Street where he was in business until 1906. John Lloyd is on the left of his bowler-hatted employee and John Jnr is second from left. This postcard was produced for advertising purposes and gives Lloyd's telephone number – 'IX'.

Nearly ninety years ago, the tailor and outfitter H.S. Whitfield knew all about the power of advertising: his hats were of the 'latest shapes', his tailoring 'superior', his prices 'modern' and all his stock 'new and smart'. His large premises in Worcester Street (occupied today by Norman Vine's and Bromsgrove Travel Centre) were substantially altered around the time of the First World War, but the business thrived here for over half a century until it was bought by Mr H.W.F. Vine in about 1929/30.

Kimberley's, the grocers in Worcester Street, in the mid 1920s. Mrs Alice Kimberley (née Lane), shown here in the doorway, lived up in Staple Hill. She had not long been married and ran the shop single-handed for a few years.

Gunner's, 'general furnishing ironmongers and cutler' in Worcester Street in 1901, with not an inch of window space wasted. The business had operated in the old Hop Pole before the inn was taken down to make way for a new road (see p. 36). Gunner's survived here until 1932.

'The Bromsgrove House' in 1960. This fifteenth-century timber-framed town house, built for one of Bromsgrove's wealthy citizens, stood on the south corner of Station Street until its demolition in 1962. An action group managed to rescue its timbers and in a giant jigsaw of an exercise these were repaired and reconstructed at Avoncroft Museum of Buildings, the museum's very first project.

Worcester Street looking south in the early 1900s, showing the overhanging solar of 'The Bromsgrove House'. On the left is the edge of the Wheatsheaf Inn and on the right are two more pubs, the Sampson Inn, just about visible directly opposite (its site still empty thirty years after demolition) and, next but one, the Dog and Pheasant, the only survivor, though much altered this century. Sam Perry was a hairdresser who also sold papers, periodicals and tobacco.

These cottages with raised thresholds in Worcester Street were photographed in about the first decade of the century. They were knocked down in the 1950s but the central building, where Joe Pinfield ran his coal business, still stands and houses the accountancy firm of one of his descendants.

The 'Anno Domini House', another timber-framed building dating back to the sixteenth century, stood at the bottom of Hill Lane, opposite Hanover Street, until it was demolished after the Second World War and the site, together with adjoining shops, cleared for housing development in 1983/4.

The Old Brewery in the early 1960s, just before it was knocked down. It stood at the rear of the Dog and Pheasant and extended across to St John Street. In the 1870s it was owned by William Bolding, who also kept the Dog and Pheasant; but not long afterwards Joseph Fitch arrived to assist him, married the boss's daughter and soon took over the whole business. Brewing, once an important local industry, was in decline by the turn of the century and the brewery closed in 1926.

Worcester Street, just after the First World War. A car advances towards the High Street but the children still feel safe enough to play and chat in the middle of the street. Bullock's, on the corner of Hanover Street, was already an old established confectioner who made 'all descriptions of ices, jellies, etc ... on the shortest notice'.

'The Olde Black Cross', Worcester Road, in the 1930s. This was a time when 'good stabling' was still an important facility for the farmers and market gardeners whose horses brought their masters and their masters' goods to market and needed to be stabled while business was transacted. The pub has been extended and restored in recent years and plenty of room made available for the horse's successor.

Hanover Street looking towards St John's Church and the Kidderminster Road. All these little houses, along with similar ones in St John Street, were knocked down in the 1950s and '60s.

Hanover Street at the turn of the century looking towards Watt Close and Worcester Road. In the nineteenth century the annual midsummer fair was held on Watt Close where, over the two days before the fair, caravans gathered, tents were pitched and stalls and booths set up. It was in Watt Close too, when the Cotton Mill's large pool froze over, that many young people learned to skate and play ice hockey.

The left hand building of this row of houses on the south side of Hanover Street (opposite today's car park) was for many years an inn, the White Hart. It had long ceased to be that when the site was cleared in 1966 to make way for the telephone exchange.

Terraced cottages on the west side of Worcester Road (to the north of Jewson's), photographed in the 1950s. The cottages were late eighteenth-and early nineteenth-century conversions or replacements of older buildings and when they were knocked down in 1960, the medieval cruck, exposed here, was rescued and presented to the Avoncroft Museum of Buildings.

Two
Around the High Street

The lower end of the High Street, west side, *c.* 1905. Camera conscious Bromsgrovians are shopping in a main street still roughly surfaced. At this stage a water cart used to pass up and down to lay the rising dust.

The east side of the High Street, looking north, probably taken from the town hall's upper storey, *c.* 1890. Mr C. Ellingworth, one of Bromsgrove's five clock and watchmakers at this period, is on the extreme right. The barrowman sitting outside the Golden Cross used to wheel the goods around to various customers of commercial travellers who were transported from the station in one of the hotel's horse buses.

The High Street, looking north in the 1920s, is by now dominated by cars. The trade van on the left belonged to Weaver and Guest whose grocery and seed business flourished until the 1960s when the owners retired. The smell of the seed and sacking in their shop opposite the Golden Cross, and of their fresh coffee in the shop a little lower down on the opposite side, is still quite vivid for some.

By 1910, the Golden Cross already had the motorist in mind. This old Georgian coaching inn had long played an important role in the town and was the chosen venue for many a celebratory dinner and meeting. Its fine balcony, from which political addresses and announcements were made, survived until 1932 when it was rebuilt by Braziers.

The back of the old Golden Cross, c. 1930. The yard, formerly used for stabling, was equipped in the rebuilding of 1932 to cater for the car and, although at that stage the pub's bowling green was relaid, it was also made to give way to the parking demands of increasing numbers of motorists.

Looking into Bayliss's yard behind the High Street in 1965. Little has changed this century. One of the narrow ancient churchways – some of them blocked off in recent years – passes through this yard and, across the High Street, continues by way of Clegg's Entry. The building on the right, the warehouse of Thomas Ince, the grocer, had just been severely damaged by fire. The three-storey building on the left was Partridge's, the butcher, until 1983.

Bayliss's yard in 1965, this time looking east towards Ednall Lane. To the left are the steps to Ince's warehouse, in the background Partridge's slaughterhouse and in the right foreground is the back wall of the butcher's pigsty.

No. 89 High Street, directly opposite Lloyds Bank, in 1966. This late seventeenth-century building is one of a group of listed buildings (Nos 85-97) in this part of the High Street. A century ago it was owned by the Adams' family, greengrocers, who sold a bit of everything and occupied the site for about forty years. The passage to the right leads to Satchwell's Yard where a former seventeenth-century inn and a smithy were restored in 1987.

Crown Close in the foreground, behind the High Street, before the cutting of the new western relief road in 1977. The passage through to the High Street is Clegg's Entry, named after the ironmonger and tea dealer whose shop stood at the top of the entry in the High Street. The building on the right was for many years Alfred Hall's workshop (see p. 103).

The earliest known photograph of the High Street, taken before 1865, when the Hop Pole was dismantled and 'moved' around the corner. It is interesting to see how many premises were still private houses.

The Home and Colonial, which was just below Woolworth's, was well established when this was taken, probably during the First World War – the portrait in the right hand side of the window is of the American President, Woodrow Wilson, who was inaugurated in 1913. The notice suggests a shortage of sugar to go with the tea.

Looking down the High Street, *c.* 1903/4. Behind the whiskered gentleman on the right is Charles Evans, bookseller and printer, who published for a time the *Weekly Independent*. The 'coffee', centre left, was available from a non-alcoholic establishment opened through local initiative to combat the demon drink and became, in the late 1880s, a branch of the Worcester City and County Coffee Tavern Company. It closed in the 1920s but gave its name to a useful short cut, Coffee Tavern Passage, unfortunately blocked off in 1986.

Dodwell's Stores, which stood below present-day Rainscourt's, in 1928. Officially listed as a wallpaper dealer, Mr Dodwell seems to have dealt in a great range of domestic items. Ten years later he had moved his business to the other side of the High Street. Unusually, this photograph was developed across two postcards and at some stage folded over – hence the crack across the centre.

The Hop Pole Inn, with its richly carved gables and unusually decorated timber frames, stood in the High Street until it was demolished in 1865. Built by Walter Brooke in the late sixteenth century, it remained in the family for two and a half centuries. Several licensees followed in its last thirty years before the Bromsgrove Town Board finally decided – despite strong opposition – that the much needed road to the station in Aston Fields (the main route, Station Street, being so treacherously steep and narrow) should start precisely where the town's finest Elizabethan building stood. The opposition, led by Dr Collis, headmaster of Bromsgrove School, had its campaign for rebuilding the inn strengthened when it was found that the Hop Pole's timbers were in excellent condition. The right hand shop in this picture is Gunner's which, on losing its premises, moved to Worcester Street.

The intricate frame of the Hop Pole, ready for auction in April 1865, was saved at the eleventh hour and acquired by the Worcester City and County Bank who, in 1866, re-erected it, with modifications, around the corner in the 'new road'. Some of the carved barge boards had to be replaced and the upper storeys reflect a more authentic rebuilding than the Victorian-influenced ground floor.

Tudor House, the former Hop Pole, before the First World War. By this time the Worcester City and County Bank had amalgamated with Lloyds who operated here until moving into the High Street in 1914. Since then auctioneers and estate agents have been in occupation. The small building, bottom left, housed the bank's vaults.

Another view of Tudor House, this time in the late 1930s, when the 'cash grocer', George Mason, was on the corner of the High Street and Woolworth's was rather smaller than today as it had not yet expanded into the premises of J.T. Taylor, the ironmonger.

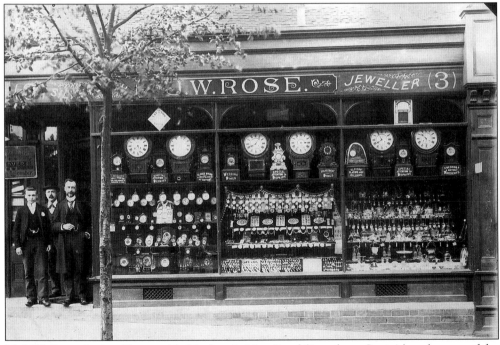

Mr J.W. Rose, the jeweller, outside his shop in New Road (just above Spain's) at the turn of the century. Mr Rose, sexton and stonemason, opened this shop in 1898 and a few years later moved to the High Street. The Rose family provided St John's with five generations of sextons. The last, nineteen-year-old John, took over from his uncle in 1879 after the latter's mysterious and fatal fall through the trap door in the belfry.

Windsor Street was laid as recently as the early 1960s. Until then the lane running off New Road behind the High Street went only as far as Chapel Street. Also demolished at this time was Windsor House, a fine private residence.

The bottom of Chapel Street in 1967. This was before the cottages – just visible at the rear of the bank – were knocked down and a precinct built.

The High Street in the first decade of this century. Behind the imposing set of whiskers on the left is an impressive eighteenth-century town house, built for a local attorney. It had a stable, a coachhouse, various outbuildings, including servants' quarters, and a walled garden. Lloyds Bank bought it from Dr Richard Wood in 1914. The children, however, are much more interested in the horse-powered vehicle.

The High Street looking north at the turn of the century. The large house, first right, was bought from Dr Prosser by Boots the Chemist in 1908. Fifty years later it was knocked down, together with the Green Dragon next door, and a new Boots built. The band of cobbles at the top of Church Street (in the left foreground) was laid to keep feet out of the mud.

Barclays Bank in the 1930s, before it was rebuilt after the Second World War. In 1915 it was known as Yardley House and occupied by John Sumner, auctioneer son of the founder of Typhoo Tea Tips. In the following year Sumner moved his business into Tudor House in New Road which today is a branch of the estate agents G&A.

The Castle Inn (extreme right) occupied part of the fine early seventeenth-century, three-gabled building opposite Mill Lane. It was pulled down in the 1930s. The banner – 'Bromsgrove Cycling Sports Bank Holiday' – suggests this quiet High Street scene was about to be transformed.

Bryant's showroom in the High Street, *c.* 1924. Bryant's originally built coaches and carriages. This old family firm was started by Philip Harvey Bryant in the 1850s, and by 1875 had moved from Stratford Road (then Alcester Road) to the High Street at the corner of Mill Lane. It had also moved into the production of cars and when the old stone Rectory Manor House was demolished, Bryant seized the chance to expand and opened a new showroom on the site. Seen here are five Wolsley cars, including one parked in the showroom's entrance. The photograph was probably taken to celebrate the acquisition of the Wolsley agency.

The Old Coach and Horses in the early 1920s. This was the last remaining 'free house' between Birmingham and Worcester. In its heyday it had stabling for around one hundred horses. It was probably the first pub to provide a lounge bar and had, apparently, a reputation for very good beer.

The yard of the Coach and Horses, around 1914. The number of 'put-up' floats would suggest market day. The notice in the centre of the picture is advertising the billiard salon with three tables. At this stage in Bromsgrove's history there were five inns between Stratford and New Roads: none survived the 1970s, although a new Coach and Horses was built on this site.

The top of the High Street before the First World War. Next to the Coach and Horses is another former coaching inn, the Roebuck, which stood on the corner of Stratford Road. It was demolished in two stages – first in 1939 and later in the early 1970s – when the very narrow road to Stratford was widened.

Griffiths' Temperance and Commercial Hotel in the Crescent (the name given to the curving stretch of High Street beyond Stratford Road). The hotel, further evidence of the effects of the Temperance Movement which began in the mid nineteenth century, was opened in 1905 and survived until the 1920s. By the late 1920s the building had become the office of the Birmingham & Midland Motor Omnibus Company, 'Midland Red'.

The Mitre Inn in 1966, before restoration. The Bromsgrove Society mounted a successful campaign to save this seventeenth-century, timber-framed building from demolition at a time – only a decade ago – when the full potential of Bromsgrove's building heritage was at last beginning to be recognized. The restoration by a private company has greatly enhanced this end of the town.

Lucy Rea in the doorway of her parents' newsagent's and sweet shop in Stourbridge Street (as it was then) in 1902. The shop stood next to the Mitre and was later owned by the Stride family for many years. Lucy worked in the shop before and after her marriage to Harold Gower and used to walk to Birmingham – presumably Bournville – to get the sweets.

The top of the town in the 1920s, showing the sweep of the Crescent. The Temperance Hotel (extreme right) has now become the Conservative and Union Central Office and the early eighteenth-century building now known as Strand House (see next two photographs) can be seen in the centre background.

Stourbridge Road, continuing round from the High Street, in the early 1900s. The cutting of the western relief road in 1977 meant the loss of buildings on both sides of the road. The dotted line (not quite on target) points to the slats in the wall of Strand House which provided the necessary ventilation when it was used as a tannery in the last century.

The rear of Strand House, No. 2 Stourbridge Road, in the 1960s. In the nineteenth century, the currier Benjamin Tandy hung out his skins and leather here. The origin of the building is rather obscure but for over a century it served as the town's first workhouse until the Union Workhouse was opened up the Birmingham Road in 1838. Between 1894 and 1964 the East Worcestershire Waterworks Company had their offices in these premises; and a couple of decades later the old established firm of solicitors, Thomas Horton and Sons, took over this extremely attractive building, having first carried out much needed restoration work.

Birmingham Road, 1965. The nearest building in the row, No. 15, was for a number of years a newsagent's run by Mrs Louisa Kings. By this time her shop had already stood empty for a few years and when it was finally knocked down, along with the adjoining nineteenth-century cottages, it was found to be a timber-framed building possibly of Tudor origin.

Just above Mrs Kings' paper shop was Manning's vegetable shop, shown here in the 1920s. Jack Manning is holding the toddler and the pony and cart was used for his 'fruit and veg' round which included the outbuildings (those not on the main site) of Bromsgrove School.

Three
About the Town

The Kidderminster Road in the early years of this century. The entrance to what was to become Sanders Park is just about opposite the horse and float.

A rear view of the Hanover Street/Kidderminster Road junction, taken in the mid 1960s when the south side of Hanover Street was cleared. Until the 1930s the workshop and premises on the left were occupied by Thomas and Edwin Grey, builders, coffin makers and timber dealers; but in the late 1980s they were demolished to make way for a doctors' surgery.

The Crib in the Kidderminster Road, just before it was demolished in the late 1950s to make way for road widening. The cottage stood opposite Church Road and was built about two hundred years ago in a dip and at right angles to the road. It was one of the town's last thatched houses and was replaced by a modern house.

Kidderminster Road looking towards the town, probably around the turn of the century – although this scene had hardly changed by 1951 when land on the right was bequeathed to Bromsgrove by the Sanders family. Miss Lucy and Miss Beatrice Sanders were the great-granddaughters of Benjamin Sanders, who established a button factory in the 1820s. For a number of years they lived with their father, B.H. Sanders, who was town clerk for half a century. They lived in Steps House (now the offices of Victor Powell, spilling over from next door, and Holt & Sellars); later the family moved to Oakdene in Kidderminster Road, now the Unionist Club, which they had built for them. Both sisters lived to an advanced age and when Beatrice died several fields were given to establish the park which bears the family's name. Beatrice, apparently, always referred to cars as carriages.

The Kidderminster Road out of Bromsgrove, with the postman stopping to pose for the camera, c. 1910. This road is still a very narrow one nearly a century later.

These two private houses in Willow Road, photographed in the 1970s, are anchored in a sea of post-war development. They were built, however, as a row of cottages – almost certainly for farm workers – in the early eighteenth century. Some alterations were made to the interiors by Victorian occupants and in this century the cottages served as the farmhouse to a dairy farm and orchards.

Rock Hill looking towards the town, *c.* 1910. On the right is St Peter's Church, opened in 1860 on farmland generously given by William Stott. Grove Farm then stretched east and south from the corner of Charford Road and the farmhouse became the first presbytery. St John's spire can be seen on the left.

Worcester Road, almost opposite Charford Road, probably in the 1960s. In the middle of the last century Francis Watt, chairman of the magistrates, lived here before moving up the hill to the Forelands, then a fine Georgian house. Many years ago, however, this attractive old house was converted into two dwellings, and the iron lattice work and ornamental eaves are long gone.

The boys are lounging around on Dyer's Bridge in the early 1920s. The bridge carried the Worcester Road over the little River Salwarpe, both road and river heading for Droitwich and beyond. The bricks on the right confirm the note on the back of this postcard, dated March 1923: 'Here's a photo of the old bridge but they are getting on with the new one.' To the left of the bridge was the pool of Moat Mill. Within thirty years this rural scene had been transformed with the building of a large council estate. The large house in front of St Peter's Church in the background is Charford Lodge.

These cottages at the lower end of Chapel Street were knocked down in 1967 and the site incorporated into a new precinct next to Lloyds Bank. They were originally the stables, coachhouse and servants quarters when the bank was a substantial private house.

Just over twenty years ago these three Victorian buildings stood near the bottom of New Road. Now the Baptist Church has been replaced, not once but twice, by modern buildings and, below it, the Cottage Hospital and the Victorian Institute and School of Art and Science, both designed by John Cotton, are now flats, though some features of the latter's façade have been incorporated into the new building.

Sunnymead, an imposing house built in the late nineteenth century, was the residence of E.B. Cotton, the auctioneer, whose offices were on the corner of Church Street (and can be seen in the photograph on p. 40). The house was demolished in the 1960s and the site is now a cul-de-sac of houses by the same name.

The Thomas White Cottage Homes in New Road, c. 1900. Built by Braziers in 1886, from money given by Thomas White who owned the Indigo Factory, this is one row of Victorian houses that has survived – but only after the trustees dealt with a threat of demolition by raising the necessary money and restoring them a decade ago.

The direct route to the station, a leafy New Road, *c.* 1912, looking down towards today's bypass. The trees have matured since its opening in 1865 but much of the land behind the road remained undeveloped for several more decades. The 'new' road was Bromsgrove Town Board's solution to problems arising out of increased trade and movement and, in particular, the opening of the railway. The mile-long route from the High Street to the station was the town's showpiece, wider and with more generous space for pedestrians. Tuesdays, however, were a different matter: on these days pedestrians and passengers on the horse buses that carried people to and from Aston Fields found they had to share the road with the cattle, sheep and pigs being driven to the station to be loaded on to trucks.

A timber-framed house in Heydon Road, Finstall, in 1965, with animal pens built under the same roof. The building was being renovated to make one dwelling when this photograph was taken.

The Stone House, photographed in the late 1950s, once stood between the Redditch Road and the railway line but was knocked down and the site swallowed up for industrial development.

The new Dragoon Inn (now the Ladybird Inn) at Aston Fields in 1905. The population of St Godwald's parish doubled between 1881 and 1901, largely due to the growth of Aston Fields, then still in the parish. The Dragoon was right in the centre of this growth and the feeling was that the old eighteenth-century coaching inn, which originally stood on what today is Banner's car park, was too small. It was replaced by this Edwardian art nouveau-style building in 1905, erected by William Weaver on the corner of the slope down to the station. Its old stables later became the workshop of the Pancheri family, artists in wood and stone, and Samuel Banner opened his butcher's shop in the inn's old premises.

Finstall Road in the 1880s. On the left is Rigby Hall gate and on the right, just in the picture, is the hazardous Skew Bridge which took the railway over this rural road. Increased traffic forced the authorities to build a new bridge in 1894 which went over instead of under the railway.

A row of cottages in Stratford Road in the late 1950s. The cottages, at the top of the hill as the road curves, were converted in the 1870s into Bromsgrove's first Cottage Hospital. When the new Cottage Hospital was opened in New Road they reverted to dwellings, but were knocked down forty years ago.

The almshouses in Stratford Road, built in 1883 to replace a row of seventeenth-century almshouses. Despite a vigorous campaign to save these attractive Victorian houses, they were knocked down in 1981 and the Methodist Centre now occupies the site.

Going, going ... These half dozen cottages in the Birmingham Road – nearly opposite All Saints Church – were deemed no longer fit to live in and, presumably, not worth restoring. A number of similar cottages in the Birmingham Road were cleared in the 1960s and '70s. This demolition included a group known as Salters Row, immediately opposite the church and, nearer the town on the same side, a longer row known as New Buildings which had been built in the early nineteenth century.

Little Heath Lane, *c.* 1950. The little parapet marks the north side of a bridge over the Spadesbourne Brook. The house was almost certainly altered over the years but the small thatched central section – a simple one-up and one-down – may well represent a peasant's 'squatter' dwelling, erected when this was part of the ancient road from Droitwich. The building fell into disuse though, as a result of the A38's gentle forking to the left just north of All Saints Church on the Birmingham Road.

Four
People

Moat Mill pool in about 1912. This area is occupied today by the Worcester Road/Charford Road junction. In *The Dreadnought* are Jack Godsall, on the right, and a relative.

Joseph and Maria Corbett in Highfield Road in the 1880s. Joseph was a nailer and, with Maria (née Pass), he lived in one of a row of ten nailing cottages in Millfields where they somehow brought up their eleven children. Maria was a strong character. Stories of her feuds over the fence with her brother-in-law and nephew reached *The Messenger:* she had hurled over a bucket of water and they had retaliated with a potato fork. She died from senile decay in 1897 at the age of seventy-three. Joseph was seventy-five when he died in the Union Workhouse from old age and exhaustion.

William Lamb at the age of ninety-six in 1906. He combined farming with ownership of the White Hart Inn in Hanover Street. In 1874 he was bailiff of the Court Leet but his most memorable experience was as a young trooper in the Worcestershire Yeomanry when he was chosen to escort the carriage of Princess Victoria and her mother as they passed through Bromsgrove on their way to Hewell Grange.

Beatrice Nokes, photographed on the occasion of her eighteenth birthday, on 18 December 1910. She is sitting with her dog at the back of her parents' shop at No. 1 St John Street (see the shop on p. 17 and Beatrice's wedding on p. 66).

The wedding day of Eithel Barrett and Arthur Carpenter, 21 March 1926, photographed outside Vine Cottage (now the entrance to Bromsgrove Rovers' football ground). The bricks at the bottom were part of the garden wall which had been knocked down the day before by a runaway horse and cart. Also in the group are, standing, from left to right: Thomas Carpenter, Ethel Carpenter and Albert (Kelly) Carpenter. Sitting: May Carpenter (née Goode) and Hilda Manning.

The wedding group of Leonard Halfpenny and Beatrice Nokes, 15 November 1916, pictured in the yard of No. 1 St John Street after a Baptist Church ceremony. The best man (between the groom and bride) is Joe Pinfield, coal merchant and later a councillor, and seated at the front are Mrs Taylor (the groom's grandmother) and Sam Willis (the bride's great uncle). Between them is little John Amess.

The wedding day of John Boycott and Annie Stiles (seated in the centre of the front row) in 1911. The photograph was taken in the yard of the Roebuck Inn, with which the Stiles family had a long association. Annie's father, George, was the innkeeper and old Mrs Stiles is the lady seated far right. In 1928 another member of the family, Mrs Elizabeth Stiles, was the licensee. The children sitting on a thoughtfully provided carpet are Peggy and George Cooper.

George and Minnie Lammas (and neighbours) outside their house in Crabtree Lane, Sidemoor, in 1907. Three of their five children are seen here: Cyril (on the chair), Gladys and Harry. Soon after this photograph was taken, the family bought some land in Dodford to farm; they built a house there and continued in their line of work, market gardening.

Moat Mill pool, *c.* 1904. On the left are Jack Godsall (in the cap) and his elder brother Charlie. The rower of the *Nancy* is unknown. J.H. Godsall, their father, was the last miller at Moat Mill in 1913, though the mill stood until the 1950s when the site was cleared for housing. The family bakery, opposite the Black Cross in Worcester Road, continued until 1979. Across the pool is Fussell and Drury's Boot Factory in Worcester Road.

Louis Weingartner at the gate of his Stourbridge Road house, c. 1920. Weingartner, a Swiss jeweller and outstanding modeller, came to England at the beginning of the century and taught in Birmingham before joining Walter Gilbert at the Bromsgrove Guild, the first of several continental craftsmen to work in Bromsgrove. He and Gilbert later left the Guild but their names are inscribed on the gates of Buckingham Palace which are the Guild's most famous work and were fashioned at its Station Street workshops.

The young William Turner and his wife outside Cherry Orchard Farm, Kidderminster Road, c. 1910. (See also p. 111.) Their two sons, Cliff and Dennis, were the farm's last tenants before it was sold in the late 1950s by the owners, the Sanders family, for housing development.

'The Cottage' on Kidderminster Road at the turn of the century, a foreign-looking corner of Bromsgrove. Known these days as Denmark House, it was built in the 1820s by Benjamin Sanders, a Worcester man who trained as a tailor and whose inventiveness led to great wealth. As a young man he moved into fashionable London circles after developing a 'ventilator', a spring fitted into the seat of a gentleman's tight breeches which allowed for more comfortable movement. A quarrel with an aristocratic client forced him to start again in America where he quickly prospered; but ill health drove him back to Europe and in Denmark he soon built up a fortune, only to lose everything at the British siege of Copenhagen. Hard times followed but eventually Sanders moved to Birmingham, the centre of button making, and then to Bromsgrove where, through an improvement to his cloth-covered button, he was able to enlarge his Sidemoor factory and employ up to three hundred people. When this photograph was taken 'The Cottage' was the home of William Corbett, the chemist and mineral water manufacturer.

Walter Nokes and family on the Kidderminster Road, *c.* 1896. Walter, the furniture remover in St John Street, died in 1904 when he was only thirty-six. His wife is pictured next to him and the golden-curled child is Walter Jnr.

Walter and Ann Rea (née Corbett) and nine of their eleven children, *c.* 1910. They were photographed at the back of their shop in Stourbridge Street (see the shop on p. 45). On the back row, from left to right are: Walter, Bob, Harry, Dick and Ash. Seated either side of Mr and Mrs Rea are Lucy and Florence; and crouched in front are Fred and Ruth. Their other son, Alf, had already emigrated to Canada, at a time when the Canadian Government was encouraging people to settle there, and four of his brothers were about to follow; each son was given £50 by their father.

Five

High Days and Holidays

Vast crowds in the High Street to celebrate the Diamond Jubilee of Queen Victoria in June 1897.

The flamboyant arch erected in the Crescent to celebrate Queen Victoria's Diamond Jubilee in 1897. The people of Bromsgrove clearly went to great efforts and decorated virtually every building. There were, however, one or two exceptions. According to the editor of *Palmer's Almanack 1898* ' ... the town hall in particular made out a strong case for demolition by allowing its accustomed hideousness to stand forth in striking contrast to the gayer buildings around'.

The Jubilee procession completed a three-mile route around the town. Almost as vast a crowd turned out in the afternoon when nearly 2,500 'school children' – almost all from Sunday Schools – had their own procession. The weather was 'very fine,' and the proceedings 'of the most hearty description' ended with a huge bonfire and fireworks display on Breakback Hill.

A remarkable photograph recording the visit to Bromsgrove of the Shah of Persia in July 1889. Formally received at the station by Mr Gimson, the stationmaster, and Lord Windsor of Hewell Grange, the Shah was escorted by Captain Everitt and the Tardebigge and Kings Norton Troops in triumphal procession down New Road beneath several decorated arches like this one.

More celebrations, this time for the coronation of George V in 1911. This is the west side of the High Street below Church Street (where the right hand group of women are gathered). The sign declaring 'LONG LIVE THE KING' (the initial letters in a different colour) was illuminated by candles held in jars between each letter.

The lower High Street on Coronation Day in 1911, and even more crowded windows and balconies than in 1897. In the foreground is the 'Hallelujah Lamp' with signs to Kidderminster and Worcester, and on the right is W.E. Perry, the clothier and outfitter, who a few years earlier had been the manager of Bradley's the outfitters.

The coronation celebrations once again, but the focus of the Market Street crowd has changed. On the left the town hall is decorated (a lesson learnt from 1897?) and under the right hand flag on the lamppost is the parapet of the bridge over the Spadesbourne. Its tablet, inscribed with the names of two seventeenth-century churchwardens, was lost during rebuilding in the late 1950s.

Austen Chamberlain, Conservative MP for East Worcestershire, addressing a crowd from the balcony of the Golden Cross on the occasion of the general election in January 1906. Despite a crushing Liberal victory in the country, Chamberlain managed to hold his seat. The ring of policemen was employed to deal with any trouble – which more often than not came from the Liberal-voting nailers. Fifth from the right on the balcony (the small white-haired man) is John Green, retired grocer, a wealthy and influential figure in the town, and said to be the first tradesman to stop living over the shop. He moved into Oak Cottage in New Road in 1879 and later built Whitford Hall.

Worcester Road looking towards the High Street on 12 May 1937, the day George VI was crowned, with flags and bunting as far as the eye can see and parking no problem at all.

Coronation celebrations for George VI and a festive Crescent at the top of the town where pictures of George and Elizabeth appear above and inside Mr Green's window. The 'Midland Red' first began operating a service between Birmingham and Worcester in 1913 and eventually built a garage in Birmingham Road in 1920. Notice the right hand advertisement for 5/- (25p) 'Anywhere' tickets.

A VE street party, 1945, in the Pleck, the bit of Sidemoor between Broad Street and Willow Road. The weather is fine and all are enjoying themselves, although the 'spread' underlines the continuing shortages. The group at this end of the table and nearest the camera are, seated on this side of the table, from left to right: Mr Faulkner, Mrs Hughes, Polly Jones, Phyllis Porter, Dorothy Ward, Lily Jones, Mocker Weaver, Henry Weaver, Edie Pearce, Esme Irish and Rene Dyer. On the opposite side of the table: George Webley, Violet Field, Nancy Fisher, Ivy Ward, Ron Kings, Alan Pearce and Gordon Loat. Standing at the back: Ron Jones (don't be deceived by his clothes!), Mr and Mrs Matthews and their baby, Daisy Loat, Mrs Webley and Mrs Wilkinson. The names of the rest of the party were too uncertain to be able to include.

Volunteers leaving for the South African War outside the Coach and Horses in 1900. The local press reported that twelve men were killed in the conflict and fourteen died from disease. Among those killed in action was Sergeant George Herbert Housman, the poet's youngest brother.

A sombre crowd watching the Territorials as they parade down the High Street in a recruitment drive in 1914. Many who answered the call – and many of those still only boys – lost their lives in the terrible four years.

A Territorial Battalion of the Worcestershire Regiment on Bromsgrove railway station before the First World War. The men were probably on their way to training camp and were being seen off by family and friends. In the background, to the right, are the Wagon Works.

The Court Leet leaving the Golden Cross, c. 1905/6. The landlord, Thomas Lander, is on the balcony, and the gentleman with the mortarboard is Samuel Saywell (see p. 84). The Court Leet is of ancient origin, a relic of a system of local government that existed for many centuries up until the nineteenth century. Its chief officer, the bailiff, still has to provide the Court with a substantial dinner.

The yard of the Roebuck Inn, 1953. The annual June fair was granted by royal charter in 1199 and the Bailiff of the Court Leet and Baron of the Manor of Bromsgrove – to give its full title – still carries out the ceremonies of 'proclamation', 'walking the fair' and conducting the Assize of Bread, Ale and Leather with the help of his aletasters, breadweighers and his searcher and sealer of leather.

The Court Leet enjoying a game of bowls in 1927. Standing, from left to right are: W.G. Gadsby (auctioneer), J.Y. Holt (solicitor), H. Woodward (driver), F.S. Jefferies (grocer), J.N. Bryant (garage owner), J.T. Taylor (ironmonger), Mr Mead (headborough, the court's chief officer), J.S. Weaver (grocer), Thomas Horton (solicitor), Mr Russell (tythingman) and William Kimberley. Seated: Albert Brazier (builder), A.E. Chappell (bailiff and auctioneer), Mrs Chappell, H.S. Phelps (skating rink and later cinema proprietor) and C. Crane (baker).

Six

School and Church

Learning through play for five- and six-year-olds in the playground of the Church of England School in Crown Close in 1939.

Crown Close, c. 1900. Its name is derived from the old coaching inn on the west side of the High Street. The close was just a small part of the twenty-six acres of glebe land which, for centuries, helped to support the vicar of St John's Church. At one time the Crown Inn's gardens and bowling green were here, as well as the botanical garden of Benjamin Maund in the nineteenth century (see p. 12). At this stage it was rented out to a local butcher for grazing his cattle. On the far left is the Jacobean-style vicarage, built in the 1840s. It became the council house after the old town hall was demolished in 1928 and was extended in 1939/40 and again in 1965/66 before becoming a nursing home in the mid 1980s. Next left is the majestically sited church of St John the Baptist, a fine medieval sandstone building, encircled by lime trees planted in the 1790s and substantially renovated in the middle of the last century. The wear and tear inflicted on the grass by the feet of the children at the National School (on the right) accounts for the very pale area.

Children and staff of the National School in Crown Close, c. 1885. The school started as a Sunday School in about 1788, moving from one building to another until increased numbers encouraged the parish to erect a purpose-built school on land leased from the Dean and Chapter. It was opened in 1833 but soon applied to join the National School Society.

A class of lively looking girls from the National School, c. 1900. There were a number of small private schools in the town but this was the one – established to educate 'the children of the poor ... in the principles of the Established Church' – where most Bromsgrove children went.

A special day for the children and teachers of the National School, *c.* 1913. They were possibly celebrating the eightieth anniversary of their first building. On the back row, sixth from left, is Lilian Nokes and the placards, held rather self-consciously, read, from left to right: 'Boarding (?) Scholar', 'Old Scholar' and 'Tardy Scholar'.

Bromsgrove College, 1908, when it was about to be sold to Bromsgrove School for use as a preparatory school. The college was first opened in 1859 in Blackmore House, Birmingham Road, by Lemuel Samuel, a Bromsgrove School teacher. It was later moved to the High Street, then finally to these bigger premises at Elmhurst in New Road; but it was Lemuel's brother, Samuel, who controlled the school for most of its existence. Also known as Saywell's Academy, its final name is perpetuated in College Road.

Bromsgrove Secondary School (now Parkside Middle School) in Stourbridge Road, *c.* 1940. It was founded in 1905 to provide boys and girls with at least a four-year education and was controlled by a board of fourteen governors. The stray chair belonged to a lady who stocked a bit of everything (including, wisely, sweets) in her little shop, just out of view, which stood next to the school long before the road was cut here.

Bromsgrove Secondary School's hockey team in the early years of the twentieth century. Standing, from left to right: M. Yardley, K. Carter, D. Lowthian, F. Jones (goalkeeper), M. Box, M. Tilt and Q. Johnston. Seated: F. Townsend, F. Young, F. Scale, J. Gibbs and E. Box. In front: B. Clegg and W. Eachus. Looking through the left hand window is M. Hodgetts.

Finstall School, *c.* 1910. This was almost certainly one class divided for the purpose of the photograph. The school was opened in 1882 and for many years was very much a family affair. Mrs Victoria Tunbridge was in charge of the infants' school from the day it opened until almost thirty-nine years later and worked until a couple of days before the birth of each of her daughters who also taught at the school. Her husband, meanwhile, was head of the 'mixed' school (older children, that is). They faced lots of problems: young inexperienced assistants, even younger and unreliable pupil teachers and monitors; outbreaks of measles, whooping cough and scarlet fever which could and did prove fatal; children starting whenever they liked – midweek, in the afternoon – and absent because of the weather, especially rain, bad roads and poor footwear, the fair, the circus, or a Sunday School outing. Despite all, the government inspectors' annual reports were consistently excellent.

The masters of Bromsgrove School in July 1906. Founded almost certainly more than five hundred years ago, it operated in the seventeenth century – and probably much earlier – in the Elizabethan town hall which was replaced in 1832. The school had virtually ceased to exist when it was rescued by a new endowment provided by Sir Thomas Cookes of Bentley in 1693.

Dormitory accommodation built on to an existing classroom and dormitory block at Lyttleton House, Bromsgrove School, 1893. In the last 120 years the site, the number and variety of buildings and the numbers of staff and students have all seen tremendous expansion and during a very long association with the school Braziers, the Bromsgrove firm, has been responsible for much of this building development.

The monitors of Bromsgrove School in July 1908; it was then a school with between 100 and 120 boys. The appointment of Frederick Hendy as headmaster in 1901 ushered in much needed changes against a more competitive background of new secondary schools and regenerated grammar schools. The curriculum was widened, new school societies started and finances reorganized to enable a start on renewing and developing the inadequate fabric of the school.

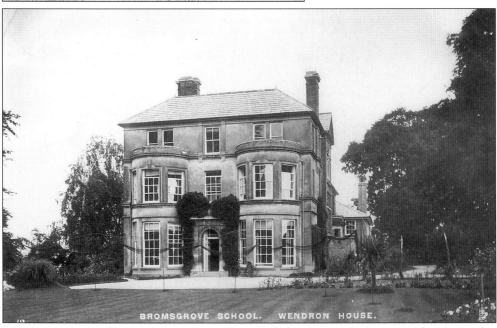

BROMSGROVE SCHOOL. WENDRON HOUSE.

Wendron House in the early 1930s. Originally called The Mount, the house was lived in at this stage by Mr A. Gillibrand, a Bromsgrove School housemaster. Boys continued to be boarded here until more accommodation was provided on the main site in the 1970s. Until recently Wendron House was the registrar's office.

St John's Steps in 1926. In 1861 the steps, which lead up to the lych-gate entrance to the churchyard, were reduced in number from sixty-three to forty-eight because they had worn so badly. Henry Hill was paid £128 to rebuild them and at the same time to remove the old lych-gate.

Bromsgrove.

The roof of St John's Church in 1926. The oak timbers of the roof of the nave were put up in the fifteenth century. In the 1920s some of the main beams were found to have decayed. Nearly all were saved, however, except one which had to be replaced – it was nearly thirty-two feet long and one and a half tons in weight.

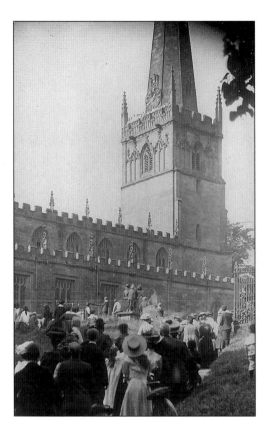

Ascension Day, *c.* 1907/8. The crowd is probably waiting for the choir to process along this side of the nave and up into the tower to celebrate the day. The girl nearest the camera with bicycle and straw hat is Kathleen Woolford.

Inside St John's Church, *c.* 1910. Behind the bishop's chair in the sanctuary is the squint, or hagioscope, which gave a view of the altar from what is now the vestry. The portraits, now moved, pictured the (then) most recent vicars, from left to right: Revd W. Villers, Revd G.W. Murray, Revd F. Paget, Revd A.E. Seymour, Revd E. Vine Hall and Revd H.D. Noel Patterson.

The second Baptist Meeting House, drawn by Revd James Ford, the minister of New Road Baptist Church, in about 1912. It was erected in 1770 in Church Street and was still standing in the 1920s, although by then it was partly a house, partly a workshop.

Moses Nokes in the 1850s. He was a member of the Baptist Church in Bromsgrove and preached at a series of cottage meetings in the Lickey and Catshill area which, until the late 1820s, had no church and was described, by Revd James Ford in *Bromsgrove Baptist Church 1666 – 1916* as 'a moral desert' where 'depravity choked the soul'. Moses was the first pastor of the chapel from its opening in 1828 until his death in 1857.

A celebratory march of the Baptist Sunday School in May 1898. In the days before the car ruled the road, and the television the home, the High Street belonged to people (and carts and horses). Crowds would gather for all sorts of occasions – the Worcestershire Hunt, an election result, the circus, a Masonic procession – and marches were frequent spectacles. The Baptist Sunday School was started by the minister, John Scroxton, in the early years of the Sunday School movement. In 1898 it had 170 children, 28 teachers and a purpose-built hall – still standing – which had been opened a decade before.

A view of the Congregational Chapel in Windsor Street, captured from a rear window of Rainscourt's in the High Street before the Second World War and nearly thirty years before the cutting of Windsor Street. In the foreground are the ivy-clad wall and pleasant garden of Lloyds Bank when it was still customary for the manager to live on the premises.

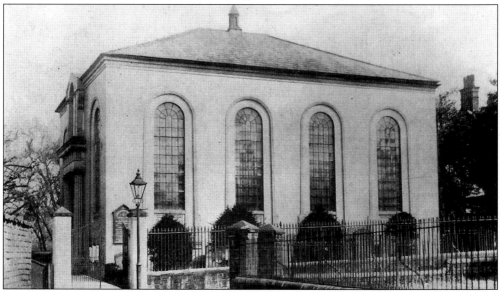

The Congregational Chapel (now the United Reform Church) in 1932. This building was erected exactly one hundred years before but Independents (as they were originally called) first met on this site in the barns of Nicholas Blick in the 1660s and '70s. The church was founded by John Spilsbury, a former Puritan vicar of St John's. The first meeting house was built in 1693, and was later replaced by the one shown here.

The women and children of Hephzibah Primitive Methodist Church (seen in the background) in the summer of 1915. The Birmingham Road church, for some years now the Royal British Legion Club, was built in 1861. The first toddler on the left in the front row is David Crane with his mother Mrs Arthur Crane. The sole gentleman, second row, is Revd Amer, with his wife on his right and daughter Betty in front of her.

A young women's class at Ebenezer Methodist Sunday School, Sidemoor, early this century. The women's married names are shown in brackets. On the back row, from left to right: -?-, Patience Chance (Wheeler), -?-, -?- and Alice Smith (Ashfield). On the middle row: Eva Crane (Robinson), -?-, Florrie Hodgkiss (Troth), Mary Jane Kimberley (Tipper), -?-, -?- and Patience Maskell (Mansell). Seated: Elsie Giles (Wheeler), -?-, Thomas Baylis, teacher, -?- and Annie Hall (Duffill).

A young men's class at Ebenezer Methodist Sunday School, early this century. Standing, from left to right: -?-, -?-, Albert Crawford, Samuel Crane, George Basil Crane, Charles Troth, -?-, Richard Duffill and Chris Chance. Seated: -?-, -?-, Joseph Pinfield (teacher), Joseph Gossage and Robert Horton. The banner shows that the 'Sabbath School' was established in 1843. Half a century later, a few years before this photograph, a new building behind the chapel had been opened for the rapidly growing Sunday School which at this stage had some five hundred members. The church itself was started in 1820 by a group of Primitive Methodists (those who claimed to be returning to Wesley's first principles) at a time when nailers – particularly Methodists like Henry Ince of Bournheath – were preaching to fellow nailers throughout the area, helping to establish chapels where there were none.

All Saints Church around the turn of the century, an Anglican 'newcomer' erected in 1874 in response to a growing population in the north of the town. The brook to the left is the Spadesbourne and council offices now occupy the fields in the foreground.

Lickey End Methodist Chapel in the early 1980s. It stood at the junction of the old Birmingham Road and Alcester Road, opposite the Forest Hotel. This attractive little building was lost when the new M42 roundabout was built in 1985.

Seven

The Working Day

The 'Midland Red' bus, Hagley to Bromsgrove route, in the early 1920s. One of the smaller companies amalgamated into the Birmingham Midland Omnibus Company, formed in 1904, operated little red horse buses; their colour was eventually incorporated into today's name.

Bromsgrove railway station with, on the right, the old milk churns ready to go, c. 1930. The station was opened in 1840 by the Birmingham and Gloucester Railway Company who chose to run the line straight up the Lickey Hills – a two and a half mile stretch at a gradient of 1 in 37.5 – instead of adopting the gentler, if longer, approach.

Bromsgrove railway station, c. 1920. The Birmingham and Gloucester Railway Company was acquired in 1846 by the Midland Railway Company which became part of the London Midland and Scottish until nationalization after the Second World War. The station was rebuilt in 1969 and the old bridge was blown up at 1 a.m. on 3 July 1988 and replaced by one that could take increased traffic from a new housing estate.

Seated on the right of this group of workers, *c.* 1912, is John Wakeman, wagon repairer at the Railway Carriage and Wagon Works which, for over a century until its closure in 1964, employed great numbers of people in the town. It came as a particular blessing to the poorly paid nailers who walked miles each day for regular employment and better rewards.

Part of the old Wagon Works in St Godwald's Road in the late 1960s. The works lay derelict from 1964 and became increasingly dangerous. Sadly, when they were finally demolished in 1981, only the balcony and footscrapers were saved from the house of James McConnell, the locomotive superintendent who was so influential in the birth of the Institute of Mechanical Engineers.

A smartly attired fire brigade, with gleaming engine, marshalled in front of the little fire engine housein Church Street not long after the First World War. The engine house stood in St John Street adjoining the vicarage wall (see p. 16). In the last century arrangements for dealing with the town's fires were less than satisfactory and in the late 1870s a new Volunteer Fire Brigade was formed with Lieutenant Hornsby as its first captain. Very soon a new fire engine was bought, similar to that used by the London fire brigade. This photograph shows the town's first motorized fire engine bought in 1919. The white-bearded gentleman seated in the centre of the front row is Alderman Job Leadbetter who served with the brigade for many years, first as a fireman, then as its captain for twenty-two years.

One of the calls made on the fire brigade on a bank holiday weekend in 1908 was by the boot factory of Victor Drury in Worcester Road, opposite Bromsgrove School. The factory had opened twelve years earlier as Fussell & Drury's boot factory, employing some three hundred people in a building that has always looked a little out of character so close to the centre of a small town.

This shows just how devastating the fire at the boot factory was. It was not very long, however, before it was rebuilt by next door neighbours, Braziers, and reopened for business in 1909.

A typical nailer's cottage and workshop, photographed in the 1960s. This one stood in Birmingham Road, Norton, until it was knocked down in 1966. There were many such cottages, most of them remaining largely unaltered until the day they were demolished. They were usually one-up, one-down and often squeezed in very large families. A few have survived and been converted into private dwellings.

A nailer's cottage, Monsieur Hall Lane, with a double-seater as its distinguishing feature, in the 1980s. In most nailers' cottages the living conditions were grim, but those who lived and worked out of the crowded town centre were usually better off because their gardens enabled them to grow food and keep poultry and a few animals.

Alfred Hall in his workshop, with his son Alfred Jnr, in about 1905. A willingness to adapt to changing times has been the secret of this family business's survival and prosperity. Mr and Mrs Hall moved to Bromsgrove in 1904 to set up a tin and coppersmith business in the small shop adjoining Whitfield's (now Norman Vine's). In a little workshop at the rear Mr Hall made dairy utensils and household goods to sell in the shop; and to make ends meet he undertook a variety of other work such as making bonnet covers for Morgan cars. When the First World War led to a shortage of steel Mr Hall dug up corned beef tins at the local tip and melted them down to make drinking utensils for poultry. In the 1920s the business moved into a small warehouse in Crown Close, concentrating on producing equipment for the poultry market. By the late 1930s a workforce of six coppersmiths and eight women assemblers was making large cooking utensils for the London trade and, when the arrival of stainless steel seemed to threaten, the business responded by moving into new areas – wrought-iron gifts, handmade copperware and hand-painted enamel boxes, luxury items which now sell all over the world.

The top of the High Street prior to 1885. The small building in the foreground is the public weighing machine office (and behind it the operator's house). It was erected in 1794 and, being much used, proved profitable to its investors until it was put out of business by a similar facility at the station. A drinking trough for horses was placed on the same spot in 1910.

One young boy and a posse of females face the photographer in the sorting room of the Worcestershire Model Laundry which stood just north of Davenal House (now the town museum), c. 1910. The building began life as Blackmore Corn Mill in 1880 but was a nail warehouse and a cycle factory before becoming a laundry in 1903 – which it remained until the 1960s.

Appleby's stand at the Two Counties Show, held in 1909, on Bromsgrove cricket ground in New Road. Nancy, the pretty girl in the picture, was the daughter of Thomas Appleby who had moved from Worcester in the late nineteenth century to take over the business on the corner of the High Street and St John Street.

Delivering coal around the turn of the century. Nadin & Co. were colliery proprietors with a head office in Worcester, a depot in Bromsgrove and agents in Stoke Road, Aston Fields (as seen here) and Rock Hill. This hard-worked horse, though not especially well groomed, is wearing anti-fly earcaps and sporting some nice brasses, rosettes and ribbons – a special occasion, perhaps.

Charford Mill (or the Lint Mill), an ancient mill rebuilt in 1875 as a boracic lint mill. In 1908 it was taken over by Southall Bros and Barclay, and prospered for many years before making way, in 1966, for what became South Bromsgrove High School. The school's ornamental pool is a vestige of the mill pool.

Whitford Mill on the corner of Timberhonger Lane, c. 1960, just before demolition. The last miller here was Harold Lammas who used it to mill oat and chaff. He later moved across the road to Whitford Farm where he died on his ninety-ninth birthday in 1991.

Roundabout House being demolished in 1899 by the employees of William Weaver, builder, contractor and timber merchant. Its removal made access to St John Street very much easier. Standing on the roof, extreme left, is William Birch, ganger, drainer and scaffolder and, second from right, bowler-hatted, is Luke Dipple, the foreman. The driver of the water cart, on the right, is Charles Taylor and the young man standing in front of the doorway, with a shovel over his shoulder, is J.W. Banner. Between the two right hand carts are a couple of Court Leet members: Henry Albutt (headborough) whose arm is resting on the tip-cart, and William Kimberley (tythingman). On the right of the picture is Appleby's ironmongery shop, its black-and white timbers still hidden beneath plastering. In front of the town hall, on the left, is one of the open-air market stands which at night were lit by kerosene lamps. The building was sold by Mr W. Llewellyn to the council in 1898 for £700.

Crown Close and Job Leadbetter's timber yard, *c.* 1895. For centuries the Crown Inn stood on this site and was the leading coaching inn entered from the High Street. The slightly taller building, at right angles to the building behind the timber stacks, was the corn exchange, built by the Crown's last owner who was forced to change direction following the coming of the railway.

Renovating the Black Cross in the Worcester Road, *c.* 1911. During the alterations, carried out by Weaver's on behalf of Cheshire's Brewery, the rendering was removed and the timber of this seventeenth-century inn exposed. The workers posing for the camera are, from left to right: Charles Lamb, -?- , Anselm Banner, Tom Tiles, Tom White, William Rollins, Eli Perry and Luke Dipple.

The last of the town hall in the Market Place, 1928. For the next half century the council would conduct its business from the former vicarage. The Playhouse, where Bebe Daniels is appearing in *Senorita* (but not necessarily in *The Chinese Parrot?*) was the converted Baptist Chapel in Worcester Road which a few years later became the Regal Cinema.

Rebuilding the open-air swimming baths in Watt Close in 1927 (see p. 123). At this point the baths were already over thirty years old. In the bath are, from left to right: A. Giles, W. Rollins, E. Lammas, E. Ashmore, T. Banner, W. Giles and B. Nash. Above: T. Lewis, J.A.H. Burford (the surveyor), Dr F.W.J. Coaker (chairman of Bromsgrove Urban District Council), W.E. Weaver (the builder), J. Hartle and W. Tomlins.

Monsieur Hall in 1938, an old farmhouse built probably in the seventeenth century and substantially altered in the eighteenth. Now a private house, it was at this stage a working farm and here Lena Hillman, the farmer's daughter, is just back from taking the milk to Bromsgrove.

Farmer Hillman standing among the stooks of corn at Monsieur Hall Farm in 1929.

William Turner of Cherry Orchard Farm, Kidderminster Road, in the 1920s. The Model 'T' Ford he is leaning on is loaded with strawberries and about to be driven to market by his son, Clifford.

GROWN WITH
CRONE & TAYLORS
MANURE

This publicity postcard from the 1930s reads: 'From MR W. TURNER, Cherry Orchard Farm, Bromsgrove. I have used your Blood and Bone Compound for Strawberries and XL Mangold Manure for Mangolds. I have had exceptionally heavy crops. I can highly recommend both manures.' The mangolds – grown to feed the animals – *do* look healthy.

Grazing cattle on land on the south side of the Kidderminster Road in the early 1920s. The position of the church and the knot of buildings near to the Kidderminster Road/Hanover Street junction suggest that the photograph was taken from the Whitford Vale direction. Some of this land was left by the Sanders sisters to create a public park.

The auctioneers' cash office (see p. 114) erected in 1853 when the new cattle market was opened. In 1978 it was saved from destruction and moved to Avoncroft Museum of Buildings where for a time it served as a ticket office.

Friar's Master and his groom in 1912, probably in Finstall Park. The groom was employed by Boultbee Brooks who moved on from designing the Brooks Cycle Saddle to becoming a very successful breeder of shire horses. The names he gave them – such as Finstall Trojan and Finstall Lady Jane – put the village on the map.

The horse fair in Church Street at the turn of the century. The annual midsummer fair attracted buyers and sellers from great distances and was a real highlight in the town's calendar. Until the middle of the last century the High Street was where horses and ponies were put through their paces for potential buyers and where deals were made on the spot. But that all changed in 1853 (see overleaf).

A busy sheep auction conducted by E.B. Cotton in October 1910. By the mid nineteenth century many had tired of the noise and dirt and damage on fair and market days, a situation considerably improved by the opening of a privately funded cattle market – on the site of today's Asda Supermarket – and by containing the sale of horses and pigs to the bottom of Church Street. In the background, right, is the Drill Hall, built in 1891, and to the left of it the instructor's house.

Empty sheep pens at the cattle market in 1965. At this stage the two small buildings in the centre were the offices of Chappell and Foster (the nearer) and Luce and Silvers (behind it). The last market was held on 18 May 1972 and with it went one of the hallmarks of this ancient market town.

Newton Farm before the Second World War. The farm was one of a number around the edges of the town which underpinned Bromsgrove's market town character. This, like many, has disappeared, knocked down after the war to make way for Garrington's factory and the houses in Newton Road.

Early nineteenth-century cottages in Charford Road, demolished in 1950 – along with Charford Farm and Little Charford Farm, almost half a mile from the Worcester Road. Charford council estate was erected on the site. In the foreground is a single-storey nailshop.

The eighteenth-century part of Cherry Orchard Farm in Willow Road and (behind) the later three-storey extension. For nearly a century and a half the farm was owned by the Sanders family until Beatrice, the last member, died in 1951 and it was sold for housing. The farmhouse itself survived for a few more years.

Strawberry pickers at Perryfields in 1897. George Lammas (with the horse and cart) rented land here and grew strawberries, supplying them to, among others, Cadbury's. His sister-in-law, Sarah Duffill, is on the far left and his young sons, Len, Harry and Harald, are at the front. This photograph could have been included in the next section, 'Sport and Leisure', but appears here because, for many, fruit picking was not so much a pleasant outing as a way of earning some vital extra pennies.

Eight

Sport and Leisure

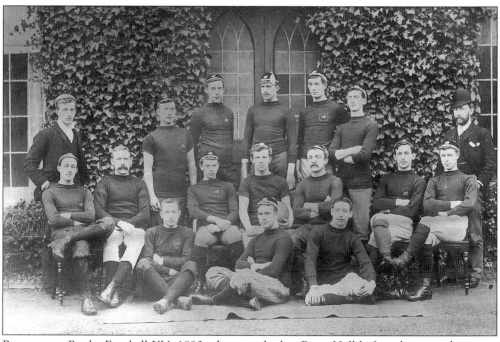

Bromsgrove Rugby Football XV, 1890, photographed at Perry Hall before their match against Stourbridge. Standing are, from left to right: E. Perkins (referee), Dr A.C. Kelp, F.W. Harvey (editor of *The Messenger*), Etienne Milward, H.B. Coney, J.E. Perkins and C.B. Hallett (honorary secretary). Seated: G.H. Housman (brother of the poet, A.E. Housman), T. Smith, G.H. Wall, C.B. Hillyar, F.S. Jefferies, H.A. Learoyd and H.A. Millington. On the front row: J. Whitecross, J.H. Milward and G. Winders.

Nurse (or Sister) Salter's dancing troupe in the late 1920s. Miss Salter, a former nurse, was a member of All Saints Church where she produced, with great enthusiasm, pantomimes, sketches and musicals, working with both children and adults. Some of the productions were taken to other local audiences like St John's and Barnsley Hall. Second from left on the front row is Edna Wakeman.

The 'Shakespearean Entertainment' advertised here for January 1889 was one scene from *King John* and three from *A Midsummer Night's Dream*. It was presented by local people, including the two Miss Sanders (who bequeathed land for the park) and two Housman brothers, Herbert, who played Starveling, and Robert, who was in charge of the 'Lime Light'.

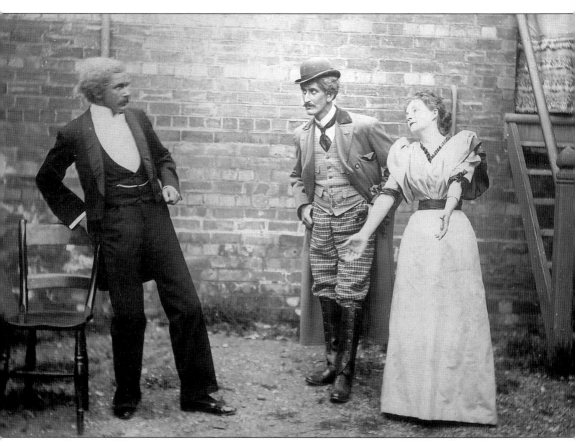

A production of the Bromsgrove Amateur Dramatic Society in 1895, which had started the year before and held its performances in the Drill Hall. In the bowler hat is J.E. Perkins. He and his brother Edward (stage manager), were well known personalities in Bromsgrove's sporting and leisure circles, with incomes sufficient to make work optional. It is perhaps surprising from our end of the century to find that very much earlier there was a choice of entertainment venues in Bromsgrove. The Drill Hall, which could seat up to 1,200, was hired out to local groups and in the 1920s changed its name to the New Court Theatre and started showing films, eventually in 1931 being re-equipped as the Plaza Cinema. There were also the Assembly Rooms and Theatre, at the corner of Stratford Road, owned by William Watton, a former gardener at St John's vicarage and a born entrepreneur. The theatre seated five hundred and many touring companies made use of it, offering music hall, variety and drama. In 1910 Watton converted it into the Bromsgrove Theatre and Electric Palace where films were shown every evening. Then there was the Playhouse which was opened before the First World War in the old Baptist Chapel in Worcester Road and later, in the mid 1920s, became the Regal Cinema.

The Bromsgrove Philharmonic Society's spring production of *King Olaf* in 1912, conducted by Mr I. Burnell. It took place at the New Court Theatre, the former Drill Hall at the bottom of Church Street which, in its final years, became a bingo hall before being replaced by an office block. The society's winter production that year was *The Messiah*.

J.S. 'Jackie' Weaver in the mid 1880s, a keen cyclist who on occasions cycled back from Cheddar where he trained for the grocery trade. His father was William Weaver, the builder, but Jackie founded the grocery firm in 1902, then went into partnership with his brother-in-law, Thomas Guest, establishing a business which survived till the late 1960s.

Cyclists outside the Horn and Trumpet, opposite St John's Church in the Kidderminster Road, in 1908. The aproned man is Thomas Cresswell, the licensee and the three bikes, from left to right, are a safety cycle, a boneshaker and a penny-farthing. It must surely have been a special event.

A mixed party leaving the Hop Pole in Birmingham Road for their annual trip to Habberley Valley in Kidderminster in about 1890. Notice how cyclists were particularly welcome.

A morning in 1919 and the regulars of the Horn and Trumpet are about to set off in two loaded brakes for a day trip to Bridgnorth. The men are mainly from Sidemoor and the left hand driver in the bowler hat is Freddy Watton who had a carriage business in Market Street. At the front with the apron is Thomas Cresswell, landlord, and on the left is his brother-in-law, Bill Hirons, and Bill's two sons, Bill and Bernard (the younger of the two). The Hirons family had not long returned from Canada where they had emigrated in 1916. Bernard remembers when the farmers tethered their horses outside the pub and when he earned a little money – a much deserved penny a time – by holding on to shire horses, terrifyingly huge to a small boy, and which, on occasions, lifted him off his feet as he clung on to their bridles.

Twelve years after the previous photograph, in 1931, the annual trip from the Horn and Trumpet is now a mixed affair and the mode of transport, a charabanc. The woman sitting on the wall, third from left, is Nellie Bird whose husband Walter was a well known plumber in the town for fifty years.

The open-air swimming baths in the 1930s, where so many learned to swim before the Second World War. Unfortunately, they were closed by the council in 1939, leaving the town without a swimming pool until the indoor baths were built in 1964. Notice the smaller boys perched on the wall on the right.

New Road Baptist Church deacons and their wives about to enjoy some tennis and golf, *c.* 1950. In the picture are, on the back row, from left to right: Mabel Sawtell, Bill Sawtell, Dennis Lott, Bert Nokes and Gerald Holden. On the middle row: Miriam Clissold, Mabel Lott, Jack Russell, Nan Russell, Gladys Nokes, Mrs Francis and Alice Holden. Seated: Alf Clissold, Marcelle Buckler, Revd Maurice Buckler, Mrs Godsall and Bernard Francis.

Eugene Humphreys, a Bank of England official and an influential figure in Bromsgrove sporting circles. As a keen young sportsman he helped to introduce the game of rugby to the town and was Bromsgrove Rugby Club's first secretary in 1872 and its captain eight years later.

Rock House on Rock Hill in the 1890s. In the centre of the group is Eugene Humphreys. He was master of the North Worcestershire Beagles for sixteen years until his retirement in 1899; and for twice those many years he was secretary of the Association of Masters of Harriers. He was also a long-serving chairman of the Higher Education Committee and the first chairman of the governors of what is now North Bromsgrove High School. The solitary female in this man's world is Miss Jocelyn Allbright of Finstall Park from whom most of the rugby club's land in Finstall was bought.

North Bromsgrove and District football league team, 1923-24. On the back row, from left to right: R.E. Griffin (vice-chairman), E. Calcutt, J. Gibson, F. Turner, V. Fisher, W. Urmaker, R. Sheriff (captain), F. Stiles and G.E. Ince (honorary secretary). On the middle row: T. Elvins, H. Husband, C. Haycock, S. Smith Esq, W.E. Whitehouse, J. Bayliss and V. Pedlingham. On the front row: R. Duggan and H. Harte.

The Bromsgrove Divisional Police Sports Club, 1927-28. The first four gentlemen seated are, from left to right: Wally de Grey, ex-Superintendent Rudnick, Superintendent Jones (president) and Sergeant Shaylor (chairman). The captain, seated at the centre of the row, is Police Constable Harris.

Bromsgrove Cricket Club 1st XI in 1913. The club is over 150 years old, one of the earliest to be formed in the Midlands. Little is known of its first few years but it was re-formed in 1861 at a meeting in the back parlour of Mr Gillespy's barber shop in Market Place and played fixtures on part of the Recreation Ground for many years. In 1907 it opened its new ground in New Road where a tennis section was started. In 1974 it played its first match on its current ground, St Godwald's Park. Standing are, from left to right: J.E. Perkins, G.W. Nicholls, W.A.H. Scott, H. Hobday, E.P.Q. Carter and -?-. Seated: Mr Stevenson (umpire), W. Hewitt, E .Perkins, -?- and Mr Hatton (groundsman). On the front row: -?-, John Kilner and -?-.

Bromsgrove School Rugby XV, 1899 – 1900. The school, still very small, had a good record at this stage although facilities were far from adequate and very few games were played. As late as 1896 the side had to be strengthened by one or more of the masters. Not until numbers increased after the First World War did there begin to be more scope for games and athletics.

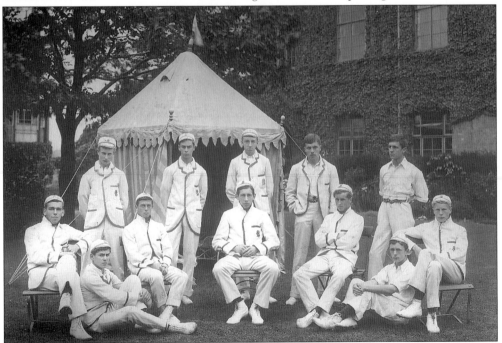

Bromsgrove School Cricket XI in 1902. Herbert Millington, who had just retired as headmaster, was very keen on games but his high standards could prove intimidating and his very appearance on the field would often herald disaster. Better times were ahead, however, starting with a new pavilion in 1905.